THE
ENGLISH EDUCATIONAL SYSTEM

BENN'S SIXPENNY LIBRARY

THE ENGLISH EDUCATIONAL SYSTEM

By CYRIL NORWOOD, M.A., D.Lit.

Headmaster of Harrow School

LONDON: ERNEST BENN LIMITED
BOUVERIE HOUSE, FLEET ST. E.C.

First published 1928

MADE AND PRINTED IN GREAT BRITAIN BY
BILLING AND SONS, LTD., GUILDFORD AND ESHER

NOTE

In preparing this short statement on a subject of great complexity, I have had occasion to consult many books and reports, but I should like to express special indebtedness to Birchenough's *History of Elementary Education in England and Wales,* Archer's *Secondary Education in the Nineteenth Century,* and Sir Amherst Selby-Bigge's *The Board of Education.*

C. N.

CONTENTS

THE ENGLISH
EDUCATIONAL SYSTEM

CHAPTER I

THE ENGLISH EDUCATIONAL SYSTEM

THIS book must of necessity be small, and the subject is vast and complicated in detail. I shall attempt merely to trace the general outlines, and refer the reader to the books on individual parts of the English educational system, which will give fuller information both about the history of the past and the details of the present than can here be attempted. Statistics will be used sparingly, for they are apt to be dull, and in a short treatise cannot be complete. The endeavour will rather be to show what is being attempted in each field, the reasons why these efforts take their present form, and the ideals which lie beneath and inspire those who teach and those who administer.

The educational system of this country is not logical, nor has it symmetry: it has not been thought out by legislators or statesmen, and imposed from above upon the nation. At the same time it is not haphazard, but it has grown from practical needs, and is now indissolubly bound up with the national life. It cannot be understood apart from the national history, for it is the product of the national character. One striking feature of that character is its capacity for making an illogical compromise work in practice, and for getting things done without bothering overmuch about theory.

We are tolerant of anomalies, and patient with
survivals, so long as they produce results that are
worth while. The history of our education is full of
instances of this genius for action and indifference to
theory, which lead our critics to belittle our thinking
powers and to represent us as a nation intimidated in
the presence of a new idea. But in practice we have
produced schools which are more powerful for the
formation of character, which awake greater and more
permanent loyalties, which provide greater scope for
individual effort than those of any other people of the
present or the past.

One general characteristic is to be noted which is
due to the mode in which education has developed in
this country. It has been inspired from above. Its
ideals have come from the Universities, and from a
few schools which looked directly to those Universities
and were closely connected with them. Its ideals have,
therefore, come from those who have been preparing
for the learned professions, for Government, and for
administration, and the standard has accordingly been
high. There is a profound difference in outlook
between a system which, as in this country and in
Western Europe generally, has begun from the Universities, and percolated downwards, and systems
which in modern times have been based on a good
system of elementary schools, and built upwards from
them. The observer will find that the general standard
of attainment is higher in the former than the latter,
and that the ideal of knowledge for its own sake, and
of pure scholarship valued for itself and for no
utilitarian reasons, is far more secure.

It has been rightly pointed out that past historical
development is the reason why education in England
is a landscape of peaks and valleys rather than that of
a uniform tableland. The work of the twentieth
century has been not to lower the peaks, but to raise
the general level of the valleys in the hope that the

inequalities will disappear. It is not often realised how recent is the growth of our educational system, or how vast and full of promise of power for the future is that wide extension of education, in the midst of which we are living. A full history, such as cannot be attempted here, would make this clear, but it will be clear enough for our purposes if we look back a century. A century is not a long time, for it covers no more than the work of three full generations, and a rapid survey of the field of education as it presented itself in 1828 will enable the reader both to measure the immense distance that has been covered, and to understand how it has come about that our system has taken its present form.

In 1828 there existed at one end of that field two Universities and a few Public Schools. Both Universities had risen considerably above the idleness and corruption which had marked them in the eighteenth century. But the Nonconformists were excluded from Oxford, and could not graduate at Cambridge. Work at a low pass level was all that the great majority of students attempted. Genuine examinations had only very recently been introduced. Jeffrey and Sidney Smith, in the *Edinburgh Review,* were whole-heartedly attacking the whole performance of the Universities. They alleged that there was idleness in the atmosphere, that Oxford neglected mathematics and taught classics in a manner which condemned it to barrenness, that Cambridge clung to all that was obsolete, and that the Fellows sought to learn nothing new, and made no contribution of their own to learning. The Public Schools proper were seven only in number, Eton, Harrow, Winchester, Westminster, Shrewsbury, Charterhouse, and Rugby, and they stood very low in public reputation. Bad feeding, bad supervision, and resultant bullying and immorality, were truly alleged against them. Their curriculum was confined to a selection of Greek and Latin authors, chosen without intelligence, and taught without conviction. The numbers in attendance were very low. Outside this group there were over seven hundred endowments for secondary education, mostly grammar schools, some classical and some non-classical, but nearly all inefficient. The mass of the nation's children were being educated, so far as they were receiving secondary education at all, in private schools, of which there must have been several thousand : they were of every grade of merit, but few were good, and many were extremely bad. Elementary education had begun, but it was largely charitable in origin, and protective and preventive in object. The Society for Bettering the Condition of the Poor was founded in 1796, the Sunday School Union in 1803, the Royal Lancasterian Institution in 1808, and the National Society for Promoting the Education of the Poor in the Principles of the Established Church in 1811. Bell and Lancaster had independently discovered how to teach on the cheap by the monitorial system, and the length of school life contemplated was from eighteen months to two years. Five years had still to pass before Parliament made its first grant in aid of elementary education (1833).

It is said that the darkest hour precedes the dawn, but 1828 would not fairly be so described. It was a period when the dawn was already breaking. Oriel College was in its great days, and if its Fellows were not so great as they thought themselves, it was producing great men such as Newman and Keble, and Arnold and Whately. The Oxford Movement was about to begin, and Mark Pattison was at the start of his career. University College, London, was founded in 1827, King's College in 1828, Durham University in 1831, and these were the pioneers of a movement which has since covered the country with a network of Universities. Arnold began his headmastership of Rugby in 1828, and from that followed directly the revival, reform, and extension of the Public Schools. Bentham and his followers were demanding popular education on democratic grounds, and Robert Owen was preaching that "the best governed state will be that which possesses the best national system of education." Whitbread had unsuccessfully fought for the cause in Parliament, and his mantle had fallen on Brougham. Nearly a million children were receiving a brief course of training in the National Schools. Brougham's Royal Commission to inquire into educational charities was sitting, and his pamphlet on "Popular Education" (1825) had gone through twenty editions in a year. The spirit of the new movement was abroad, and already self-conscious, but hampered by vested interests in Church and State, by natural indifference, and by its own ignorance of the best way in which to advance.

Some Books for Reference

Adamson: *Outline of English Education, 1760-1902.* (Cambridge University Press.)

Archer: *Secondary Education in the Nineteenth Century.* (Cambridge University Press.)

Board of Education Annual Reports for 1908-09, and 1923-27.

CHAPTER II

ELEMENTARY EDUCATION

As has been seen, voluntary agencies were first in the field, and the State lagged behind. It is probable that the State would have frankly and fully taken up its burden much earlier if it had not been for interdenominational jealousy, as some call it, or the difficulty, as others would say, of providing for sound religious teaching. At any rate, owing to this religious difficulty, successive governments, Liberal and Conservative, failed both in 1839 and 1843 to solve the problem, and having burned their fingers left the work to the volunteers, and mainly to the Church of England. By the middle of the nineteenth century a great denominational system, training nearly two million children in elementary subjects, was established, though its imperfections may be realised when we remember that a large number of children were in no school at all, and those that were in school attended generally for less than 100 days a year, and left at the age of eleven. A Royal Commission, which sat from 1858-61, reported that there were 573,000 scholars in private schools, 671,000 in denominational and factory schools, receiving no public grant, and 917,000 in schools, mostly denominational, and in receipt of grant. It was with this situation that the Act of 1870 dealt. It accepted the facts of the case, sought to fill in the gaps, and to provide a certain equality of opportunity. The voluntary schools belonging to the various denominations were recognised and encouraged, while it was enacted that in areas with inadequate or unsuitable provision, Board schools might be set up by local bodies, elected for the specific purpose, and authorised to raise a local rate not exceeding 3d. in the pound.

Progress became more rapid, and in six years the number of school places was doubled. Compulsion to attend became possible, and between 1876 and 1900 the requirement of attendances was increasingly enforced. In the latter year, authorities were enabled to raise the age of compulsory attendance to fourteen. The policy of payment by results was tried, condemned, and abandoned. It had begun with the revised code of 1862, and had developed into a system under which an inspector tested all the pupils once a year, and the fortunes of the teacher depended upon the result. It led to cram and mechanical teaching, discouraged experiment, and enforced a wrong system upon the schools. A system under which an inspector could solemnly report that " the mental arithmetic of the junior babies left much to be desired " stands self-condemned, but it left its mark on the schools for more than a generation.

The gradual raising of the age to fourteen made it increasingly clear that there were many children in the elementary schools well qualified for more advanced education, and attempts were made towards the end of the nineteenth century to provide for these by scholarships to the secondary schools, and by " Higher Grade " elementary schools, first established in 1894. Even for Englishmen a system by which elementary schools gave secondary instruction was too illogical, and the " Cockerton " judgment of 1901, which declared the expenditure of the London School Board for this purpose to be illegal, brought that solution of the difficulty to an end. But the problem existed, and had to be faced. Other attempts of the School Boards, such as the provision of higher elementary schools with an age-range of 10-15, and of Pupil Teacher Centres, only served to show that the problem was greater than with their powers they could solve.

The situation in 1900 had become difficult in other ways. The burden on the voluntary schools had been steadily increasing, and it was becoming increasingly clear that fees for elementary education would have to be abolished. In 1891 free schooling had been made possible, and in the next ten years was made a reality by many School Boards : yet without fees many voluntary schools could hardly carry on. The School Boards themselves, directly elected to perform a limited task in a field where co-ordination is necessary above all things, were proving unequal to their task, and were in any case far too numerous. In 1900 there were existing 3,351 separate and independent authorities for elementary education.

It was a period when it was rightly believed that centralisation and unification of control were necessary if efficiency was to be achieved. The Board of Education Act of 1899 had united the Departments of Education, and of Science and Art, and conferred on it the educational powers of the Charity Commissioners. The Education Act of 1902 which followed is a great landmark in educational history. It replaced the 3,351 independent authorities by 328, and made education a function of local government and an expression of local patriotism. It made possible the establishment of secondary schools, wholly maintained by public money, and in many areas it set up a single authority charged with the provision of all types of education. It took over the cost of secular education as one which fell entirely upon public funds. But great as was the advance which it made possible, it left untouched some abnormalities, nor did it remove the dualism which we owe to our religious denominations. It obliged the new local authorities in all cases to supply and control elementary education : it empowered the county councils and county boroughs to provide technical and higher education. Thus it put county boroughs in control of all their education, with power to co-ordinate it, but it excepted from the authority of the county councils all the borough and urban districts with a population above 20,000. Thus, in many areas elementary education remained, and remains, under the control of several authorities, while higher education is under one. The Act left the buildings of the voluntary schools in the possession of the denominations, and the religious teaching of the schools under the authority of the school managers, who retained the right to appoint the teacher. All these anomalies left by the Act of 1902 still remain, and in varying degrees impede the course of educational reform.

Nevertheless, the Act removed many obstacles. The relation of elementary to secondary education began to be more fully explored. Continuation, trade, and vocational schools began; secondary schools were increased in number. In 1907 it was made a condition for the receipt of full government grant by a secondary school that it should admit 25 per cent. of its scholars as free places from the elementary schools, though, in practice, anything from 10 to 25 was taken as fulfilling the law. Denominational feeling was, indeed, strongly aroused by the Act of 1902, and various attempts by Mr. Birrell and others to find a way of reconciliation were made and failed. That feeling may now be considered to be dormant rather than extinct, and probably every year that passes makes its revival in the old intense form less likely. Statesmen, however, for the present, continue to prefer to put up with an inconvenient dualism rather than attempt unification at the cost of religious strife.

The feeding of schoolchildren was made possible by the Act of 1906, and medical inspection by the Act of 1907. Under these, and especially the latter, a great work has been accomplished, and it has been supplemented by a more enlightened system of physical training, and the work of voluntary After Care and Juvenile Employment Committees, which began in the period before the war, and have done much to humanise the treatment of children, and to state and face the problems that are before them.

The war did much to increase the national sense of the value of education, if only for its testimony to the superiority of educated soldiers over illiterate masses, however brave. It led immediately to further legislation, and the Fisher Act of 1918, however much high hopes have since been dashed, remains the charter of free elementary education. That Act, and the Education Act of 1921, have improved the salaries of teachers, given them pensions, and bestowed more liberal grants. Fees have been abolished, "half-time" forbidden, and attendance has been enforced up to the age of fourteen with the possibility of further extension. A frank partnership has been entered into with the local authorities, in which the initiative is handed over to them, and the preparation of ambitious schemes for development over periods of ten years has been encouraged. But on all this there fell a sudden blight, when the slump in trade occurred, and the national finances were found to be in difficulty. Projected schools were abandoned, the raising of the school age deferred, salaries were reduced. There was embittered altercation between economists and educational reformers. Perhaps the pause has been no bad thing. The nation was embarking on a number of schemes which would have proved expensive and had been insufficiently thought out. The cessation of active expansion has enabled educationists to do some quiet thinking, and the result may well be, when the opportunity arrives, the creation of an education which is really national and really a system.

It is not so very long ago that elementary education was thought to be something fit and proper for the sons of the labouring poor, secondary education, if not too long continued, a suitable privilege for the middle classes, and University education the proper sphere of the rich, so long as the deserving and clever poor boy was enabled to make his way there by aid of scholarships. There are now many who see that elementary education is that which lies at the foundation of the whole, covering for all children the years from their second to the eleventh. The nursery school, the infant school, and the junior school are stages within the range of those important years. From the eleventh to the sixteenth or eighteenth year lies the province of secondary education, and it is realised that all who come up from the elementary stages need proper and suitable provision. It is here that the great gaps are found which prevent the English system from being really adequate to its full work, but a study of the defects may well be deferred until we have considered all the forms of education at present existent. Full provision for the nation's need can only be made by authorities dominant for the purpose over all types of education throughout large areas, and that full provision will be expensive. But all the omens go to show that in due time and with due consideration this full provision can be made, and that it will be made.

Eighty years ago Macaulay, referring to common schoolmasters, spoke of them as " discarded footmen and ruined pedlars," and our literature is full of terms of contempt for the humble pedagogue. The eighty years which have elapsed since Macaulay passed his judgment have brought higher status, better training, increased knowledge, and more adequate income. There were in 1925 165,047 teachers in elementary schools, an army in themselves, and the most valuable social service which we possess. Their training has greatly improved. Not so long ago it was carried on in sordid surroundings under monastic conditions: neither air nor variety nor exercise were thought necessary for the future teacher. It was thought that he would thrive best on a consumption of textbooks for knowledge, and sectarianism for religion. But now many types of training are open to him, in a University or University college, or in a denominational or municipal college. The ideal for the future elementary teacher is that he should follow the ordinary school and college course in the company of those who will seek other occupations. Early segregation is certainly bad, and the spirit of the seminary is to be avoided. It will probably become more and more the custom to attach the colleges for the training of teachers to some University, and to endeavour to give them a tutorial staff. And it is to be hoped that future teachers will increasingly give three years to a course of study for a degree, and follow it with one devoted to professional training. It is better to have a wider equipment of general knowledge and a less intensive course of pedagogy than to pass through a long period of class management and class training on a very slender stock of knowledge and a very imperfect education. It should surely be sufficient, if a compromise were effected between the over-training of the elementary teacher and the under-training of the secondary teacher, if the former were trained less and the latter more. It is a wise suggestion that the difficulty of practical training should be met by making the first year in the elementary school probationary, and causing it to be spent under supervision, and thereafter that professional knowledge and technique should be renewed and increased by the institution of summer schools and refresher courses.

A generation ago unattractive conditions of training and poor prospects combined to make the output of trained teachers very low, and quite inadequate to meet the demands of the national service. In 1890 only 2,791 trained teachers were produced. But by 1914 this number had risen to 12,000, and by 1920 to 13,500.

Under the conditions of training now available, and with the improvement in salaries, pensions, and status, a supply of good material is available, and should steadily be forthcoming.

It may naturally be asked at this point: " What is actually taught in an elementary school, and how are the teachers equipped?" To take the latter question first, the teachers have as the basis of their training a knowledge of English, history, geography, elementary mathematics, and science, to which they can add certain optional subjects. They are trained in the elements of exposition, class management, hygiene, and psychology. The schools have become more free and more individual, thanks to the passing of a generation during which they have been free from the tyranny of the three R's, rigidly conceived, and the system of payment by results. The study of formal English grammar has declined, and the old-fashioned readers have given way to the use of literary readers of good prose and poetry, supplemented by the reading of recognised authors in whole or in part. Supplementary reading in history, geography, and nature study is encouraged: school libraries and travelling libraries are in use in country districts, and in towns and cities the use of the municipal library is encouraged and directed. The study of arithmetic has been widened to include the elements of mensuration and of simple algebra and geometry. Physical training has been reorganised, and the place of hand and eye in education has been realised. Handwork and carpentry are regularly taught, and drawing now includes the use of several media—pencil and pen and ink, pastels and paints. Subjects have not so much increased in number as received each a new and wider treatment. Children, for instance, in English not only read aloud and learn repetition, but are encouraged to compose aloud, to speak, and to read for their own enjoyment. Geography is so taught as to be a study of causes and

effects, and of how to read, understand, and make a
simple map. Pictures and acting are brought in to help
history, nature study and practical gardening to help
elementary science. Needlework means not the pro-
duction of specimen samplers, but household work
and a knowledge of stitches and ordinary garments.
Besides this, all, both boys and girls, have lessons in
singing, in physical exercises, and in hygiene.

The London Education Service of 1927 gives the
following as a typical "time-table" of an upper
standard in a London elementary school:

Lessons.	Hours per Week.
Bible instruction	2½
English (including reading and writ-ing) and arithmetic	10
History, geography, singing, and dancing	5
Science and practical work (including needlework and domestic economy for girls, and woodwork and metal-work for boys)	5½
Physical education	1½
Play intervals, registration, etc. ...	3
Total	27½

There have been a good many movements in education in the last twenty-five years, and most of them
have had their reactions on elementary education.
Some of them have led in the direction of a break-
away from ordinary class teaching, and of these the
most influential has been the Dalton Plan, which came
from America. Briefly, this method conceives of pupils
divided into small groups, devoting their time con-
tinuously to one subject at a time, and helping one
another to make the study effective. Discussion, read-

ing, consultation of books, are carried on by the pupils themselves with only occasional guidance from a teacher. It is claimed that the method promotes teamwork, a sense of freedom, and the spirit of co-operation. At an earlier stage the influence that comes from Italy, from the teaching and example of Madame Montessori, has also made for freedom. That the child shall do what it wants to do, and that the teacher should use what the child wants to do, as the best means for its education, that the education consists in providing the best opportunities for individual development, are principles that are steadily gaining ground. From our own country, from the writings and example of Miss Charlotte Mason, who founded the Parents' National Educational Union, and conducted a model school at Ambleside, has also arisen a movement for securing the co-operation of class with teacher and for emphasising the same principle of freedom and self-education. The exponents of her method claim that they secure and maintain the interest of the pupils; and certainly in the hands of good teachers remarkable results have been obtained, in the elementary schools of Gloucestershire and elsewhere, and in preparatory private schools.

A good many people are apt to decry the product of elementary education, and in particular to allege that the old accuracy in the three R's has been lost and a sloppy impressionism substituted. Such people forget that the accurate exponents of arithmetic and spelling, who used to be found in the elementary schools, have now found their way with scholarships and free places to the secondary schools, and that in most cities and towns the elementary schools in the highest standards have more than once been skimmed of their cream. But if anyone doubts whether progress has been real, he need not rely on written argument or the consideration of conflicting opinions. He will be converted if he looks at photographs of elementary school classes taken at intervals of twenty years. In the pamphlet called *The London Education Service*, issued from the County Hall, there is a photograph of the infants' class at the Oratory School, Chelsea, taken in 1905, and again in 1925, and of a class in an infants' school in Southwark in 1894 and again in 1924. These are more persuasive than many pages of discussion. The look of the face, the carriage of the body, the eye, the mouth, the hands, all tell the tale of improvement to those who look closely. It is not only treatment outside the classroom, but better and more humane methods inside the classroom that have combined to bring about this result.

There is in progress throughout the country an unequal, but still a general, movement towards the reduction of the size of classes. Classes of not more than 40 in the case of infants, and 48 in the case of older pupils are aimed at, and these, as soon as they are realised, bring with them the opportunity of better methods and an altogether higher type of education. At the start, when classes were huge, parents indifferent and hostile, and the child mind not studied, discipline and mechanical accuracy were all that could be secured. Now the elementary schools set themselves to do no less than impart the elements of culture. They rely mainly upon English as a written language and a spoken tongue, and on the cultivation and training of the hand, the voice, and the eye. Dr. Ballard, one of the London County Council's Inspectors of Schools, has said : " If the great discovery of the nineteenth century was the human hand, the great discovery of the twentieth century was the human voice—the discovery that by cultivating the tongue we are at the same time cultivating the mind." Speech, song, elocution, acting, all now have their place.

This chapter must not be closed without reference to the infant schools of this country, which, taking the children into the system of public instruction at five, a year earlier than any other country, have developed an institution of individuality and peculiar merit. The note of the infant school is freedom and individuality, the children are not passive, but active, doers and not mere listeners, happy and not suppressed. The new methods have spread beyond the elementary school proper into the preparatory private schools, and everywhere in the country now it is possible to see classes of tiny children thoroughly enjoying school and manifestly profiting by it. There is certainly no more pleasant sight in the whole field of education.

Those who wish to know more about the many-sided activities of elementary education at the present day should consult works specially devoted to the subject. It is impossible to discuss them fully here. There are here and there schools with special curricula, devoted to practical work in very poor neighbourhoods, schools for nautical instruction in dockside districts, and for gardening and work on the land where the children come from the land. There is a hopeful movement towards organised games, and the provision of playing-field facilities. There are school journeys and educational visits, and the coming-in of broadcasting and the use of the cinema. Much more might be said about music and art. Much might be said about the whole subject of the treatment of the defective, divided in London into eight types—blind and partially blind, deaf and partially deaf, mentally defective, and physically defective, tuberculous and epileptic. Much ought to be said about the general organisation of After-Care. The impression which a study of the whole subject gives to the observer is that the situation is full of hope, that great things have been accomplished, and greater achievements await us, that we have a splendid body of teachers, and good material upon which they can work. There are defects and gaps in the general system, but they are such as better organisation, patience, and, it must be added, the expenditure of more money, can certainly remove.

SOME BOOKS OF REFERENCE

Board of Education Annual Reports for 1910-11 *and* 1912-13.

Birchenough : *History of Elementary Education.* (University Tutorial Press.)

Sadler : *Our Public Elementary Schools.* (Butterworth, 1926.)

Lynch : *Individual Work and the Dalton Plan.* (Philip and Son.)

Montessori : *The Montessori Method.* (Heinemann.)

Jones : *Training of Teachers.* (Oxford University Press.)

The Teaching of English in England. Board of Education Report, 1921.

Circular 1350 of 1925.

CHAPTER III

SECONDARY EDUCATION

A. REVIVAL AND EXTENSION OF THE BOARDING-SCHOOLS

IT was remarked in the first chapter that the old boarding-schools a hundred years ago were in a bad way, both in numbers and prestige, and also that a hundred years ago Arnold began his headmastership of Rugby. So far as one man was responsible for the revival and reinvigoration of the boarding-school system, that man was Thomas Arnold. It is fashionable among those who for various reasons dislike and distrust this system to belittle Arnold, and even to speak of his work as a myth. But the fact cannot be denied that after his headmastership all was changed: the old schools were one by one reformed, and new ones founded on the same model. Nor can it be denied that he made a reality of the prefect system, trusting his Sixth and moulding it by his personality, that he modernised and widened the curriculum by introducing French and mathematics as regular subjects, and by teaching history in a living way, and that he saw the proper use that could be made of organised games. Further, he made the chapel the centre of his appeal to the school, a thing which before his day had not been done.

It so happened that his work fell at a time when a larger demand was rising for the sort of education which had hitherto been mainly aristocratic. The middle classes were making their way to power, and seeking equal privileges for their sons. Railways were being built, and transit was becoming easy. Wealth was growing, and there was a very large increase in the number of those who were earning up to a thousand a year and beyond. The service of the dominions beyond the sea and foreign trade were augmenting the number of those who, compelled to live abroad, yet demanded an education at home for their sons. As a result, a large number of schools came into existence, which were boarding-schools on the old model, as interpreted by Arnold. Some were old foundations, half derelict, but converted by the headmasters from the service of a purely local to that of a national field. Others were completely new, and specifically devoted to the education of the sons of a particular class, as Marlborough for the sons of the clergy, or Wellington for the sons of officers. If any-one were to go through the list of the great boarding-school he would find that, apart from the seven already mentioned, they have nearly all found their origin in their present form in a space of about twenty years in the middle of the nineteenth century, beginning with Cheltenham in 1841 and ending with Malvern in 1862. Since the war the inability of the existing schools to accommodate all who seek to go to them has led to further extension, and Stowe is only the best known of a group of several schools which have been quite recently established on the same model.

The question is often asked, "What is a Public School?" and it is one to which it is impossible to give a clear answer. It is a term supposed to apply especially to the great boarding-schools, and in popular use it is frequently confined to them. But this use is not justified. The great day schools, such as St. Paul's, Merchant Taylors', King Edward's, Birmingham, Manchester, Bristol, Bedford, Grammar Schools, have all been in the great tradition. A Public School is one which has a real measure of independence, and can direct its own policy, which keeps its pupils to the full limit of age of eighteen and over, and which has a direct and regularly maintained con-

nection with the Universities. It is obvious, therefore, that every school may aspire to this status, and
realise it, and that any school may drop out of it.

Just because of their independence, these schools
are of peculiar value, for they are the spheres of
influence of remarkable men, prophets of their
generation, who can work out unhampered the ideal
which possesses them. Moberley of Winchester,
Vaughan of Harrow, Thring of Uppingham, Bradley
of Marlborough, Benson of Wellington, Percival of
Clifton, Almond of Loretto, Sanderson of Oundle
are examples of the truth that a great work for education can be done under these conditions. In a great
State system of education it is probably vital to its
health that there should be a group of schools which
stand outside it, where experiment can be tried, and
personality find expression. It is worth while to recall
that Thring gave six reasons against State-maintained
education : (1) That it places the ignorant community
in the position of judge; (2) that it places the skilled
teacher under the power of the ignorant official;
(3) that experiment and improvement are prevented
by the regulations of authority; (4) that new types of
school cannot be started by individuals who have new
ideas; (5) that it destroys interest, since people are
indifferent to that for which they do not pay; and
(6) that it is undenominational, and no undenominational education can be really religious. The case
has gone against Thring, and we have now a great
State-aided system of education, doing work which
he would have been the first to value, had he lived
to see it. But there is enough truth in the objections
which he urged to show that it would be a disaster
to sweep away all independence from our national
provision, as some doctrinaire system-mongers would
like to do.

As things stand to-day, a public boarding-school is
usually a school of from 450 to 750 boys (though Eton

is considerably larger than this), divided into Houses, in which the House-master stands in close personal relation to each boy. They generate an intense school feeling, and often a still intenser "House" feeling. The curriculum is much the same as that of other schools in the secondary system, save that Latin holds a stronger position, and science is begun later. Their enemies say that they make a fetish of games, and their friends that they realise the value of games in the building of character, as a moral safeguard, and as an instrument for founding physical health, strength, and grace. They teach boys self-government, and they inculcate the spirit of service. They seek to make the chapel the centre of a definite religious appeal.

They are much studied by observers from abroad, and are the centre of incessant controversies at home. They are the most individual institution of all that this country has created in education, in their merits and their faults the most English. They awake strong hostilities, but intenser loyalties. At their best they have much to give to national education, the tradition of friendship between teacher and taught, the tradition of discipline and loyalty, the tradition of co-operation, and government for the good of the governed, the tradition of service and of the religion which proves itself by its practical fruits. But they are confined to the children of the well-to-do, and neither masters nor boys have sufficient contact with the rest of the national system; for it is clear that social prestige can become snobbery, and isolation can become exclusiveness, and segregation can establish caste.

Beneath these schools, and supplying them, are several hundred private preparatory schools, many of them very efficient, some too luxurious, and some incompetent. It is the most favourable field left for private adventure, and it invites equally the prophet and the charlatan, for anyone may start a school. On the whole, the work of these schools is conscientious, and in some of them remarkable personalities have given their lives to the well-being of boys from nine to fourteen. But their work tends to be dominated too much by the requirements of the Common Entrance Examination, which has to be passed by nearly all the boys who would enter the great boarding-schools. This tends to cram and mechanical and unintelligent teaching, so that the sons of the well-to-do are now suffering from the very evils which were rightly discarded from the elementary schools of the people towards the end of last century, when payment by results was abolished.

B. Secondary Education during the Nineteenth Century

The nineteenth century was a period when there was much talk about secondary education, but remarkably little was done. There must have been in existence when the century began some 500 endowed grammar schools, and a large but varying number of private schools. Some were wealthy; most were very poor; practically all had been neglected. Their distribution bore no relation to population, and their resources bore no relation to their needs. The Schools Enquiry Commission of 1864 recommended that their finances should be reformed, and that authorities should be set up with power to supplement existing schools. The first recommendation was carried out, and led to a valuable revival of existing schools, but the second was neglected, and nothing was done. Hence arose the need on the elementary side to provide some sort of secondary education for the best schools, and the experiment of those higher grade schools which was stopped by the "Cockerton" judgment of 1901, already referred to. Hence, also, as a side development of the Technical Instruction Act of 1889, there came into existence what were known as Organised Science Schools, which devoted an excessive amount of time to science and art, but represented a genuine attempt to give secondary education. Finally, Pupil Teachers' Centres were started to educate the future elementary teachers from fourteen to eighteen. In the last ten years of the nineteenth century all these were in existence, together with a large number of preparatory schools, and schools founded by religious bodies and by companies. Not unnaturally, Lord Bryce's Commission in 1894 posed the question, " How can the sporadically created and unorganised secondary education of England be organised into an efficient and satisfactory system?"

C. Progress since 1902

The Education Act of 1902 empowered county and borough councils to establish and maintain secondary schools, and little by little the new authorities were drawn into taking interest in secondary education, and the existing and struggling secondary schools learned to lose their fear of the newly created authorities and the Board of Education. By 1904 the Board was able to issue its first Regulations for Secondary Schools, and it defined a secondary school as that which offered to its scholars up to and beyond the age of sixteen " a general education, physical, mental, and moral." It required a four-year course, which should embrace English, geography, history, at least one language other than English, mathematics, science, and drawing, together with manual work, physical exercises, and, for girls, housewifery. In 1907 the Board removed inequalities by fixing a uniform grant of £5 for all pupils between the age of twelve and eighteen, and sweeping away the preferential treatment of the

organised science schools. But they imposed two conditions—that the majority of the governing bodies should be representatives of popularly elected authorities, and that the schools should offer 25 per cent. of their places free to ex-elementary schoolchildren.

It would have been, perhaps, better at that time if the State had been more generous and provided the schools with greater means to meet their new obligations. The cost of the free-place system took away the benefit of the increased grant, and what was needed at the time quite as much was the improvement of the salaries of those who taught in secondary schools. But with much searching of heart the schools, on the whole, faced up to the new position, and the free-place system may be said to have justified itself. The free places have become virtual scholarships, and brought into the schools excellent pupils, who remain at school for a longer period than the fee-paying boy. These boys have in a very few years considerably strengthened the fifth and sixth forms, sparsely filled in old days, and many of them have become school-leaders. More than 30,000 such pupils are now being admitted free to the secondary schools each year, and there were in 1925-26 134,177 in attendance.

The period up to the outbreak of the war was one of quiet and solid, but by no means rapid, development. The more progressive authorities surveyed their means, noticed the gaps and the weak places, and made plans to supply the deficiencies. The main struggle of the period was to secure an earlier age of entry to the school, and at the same time to extend the school life; for the four years' course assumed by the Board's regulations was a four years' course only in theory. What results were secured may, perhaps, be best judged statistically. The average school life went up in the case of boys from 2 years 7 months to 2 years 9 months, and in the case of girls from 2 years 7 months to 3 years; the average leaving age of boys was

2

15·7, and of girls was 16. In 1904 there were 575 schools for boys, for girls, and for boys and girls, and in 1914 1,047, the pupils in attendance had gone up from 97,698 to 178,884, and the number of pupils per 1,000 of population had risen from 2·9 to 5·5.

The war changed the situation. Whatever the cause, it brought with it an intensified desire for education, and it provided large sections of the population with the means to pay for it. Nor was it a passing desire. It warmed suddenly into life a growing appreciation of the value of education which had been steadily gathering force under the surface. This demand, while embarrassing to the schools because of the numbers who clamoured for admission and could not be accommodated, nevertheless enabled them to set their houses more in order, to cut down their purely preparatory departments, to secure a standard of attainment and a proper age for entry, and to increase school life. Again the progress made may be measured statistically. The average school life in 1924-25 had risen to 3 years 8 months in the case of boys, 3·9 in the case of girls, and the average leaving age to 16·1 and 16·3 respectively. The number of schools had increased to 1,301, and the number of pupils in attendance to 367,564. The average size of schools, which had been 190 in 1914, was in 1925 283. The number of pupils per 1,000 of the population is now practically 10.

But the main progress was made in strengthening, and providing for the maintenance of, good work at the top of the schools, and creating sixth forms of respectable numbers. Advanced work had engaged the attention of the Board from 1913 onwards, but progress became really possible when Mr. Fisher in 1917 offered grants of £400 a year for each advanced course which a school could maintain. These were, and continue to be, mainly for science and mathematics, classics, and modern studies, though combinations of these, and geography, have recently appeared. In 1917

there were 82 such courses recognised in science and mathematics, 20 in classics, and 25 in modern studies; in 1925-26 these had become 283, 38, and 189 respectively, apart from 15 others of varying types. In other words, in nine years the advanced courses had nearly quadrupled in number, the most satisfactory evidence that can be offered that the work of the secondary schools as a whole has greatly improved in quality.

In a period of less than twenty years, again, the number of boys proceeding from a secondary school to a University has more than doubled, and the number of girls has more than trebled. And, on the other hand, the newer Universities are set free from the burden of doing elementary work with which they used to be vexed, for it is done in the schools. No University now admits any student who has not matriculated.

Space does not permit of a description of the chaos of examinations which afflicted the secondary schools during the nineteenth century. It must be enough to state briefly the system which, as the result of long consideration and many efforts, is now in force. There are two examinations approved by the Board in secondary schools. The first is for pupils about or just above the age of sixteen. The subjects are divided into four groups : (1) English subjects, (2) languages other than English, (3) science and mathematics, (4) a group of subjects outside the main curriculum, such as music, art, carpentry, domestic science. Every candidate must pass in each of the first three groups. The second examination tests work at a stage two years later, after specialisation in the advanced courses, and is designed for sixth form work of a good standard. These examinations are conducted by eight examining bodies. The school certificates gained at the first examination may exempt from matriculation and from the preliminary examinations of professional bodies.

They have also a definite value in the commercial world. The higher certificate may, under conditions, exempt from University intermediate examinations, and is freely used for the award of scholarships. The whole system is under the general surveillance of the Secondary Schools Examinations Council, established in 1917. In that year (1917-18) 14,232 candidates took the first examination and 550 the second; eight years later the numbers had become 43,092 and 6,380, and they are still rising steadily.

There has therefore been a great and very rapid advance in secondary education during the present century, and the causes have been so admirably summed up in a pamphlet issued by the Board of Education in 1927, " Recent Development of Secondary Schools in England and Wales," that it seems well to close this chapter by quoting it.

" (a) First and most fundamental among these (causes) stands the new fact of public control, without which none of the other developments would have been possible.

" (b) Directly dependent on this stands proper financial provision, both for building and maintenance.

" (c) The regulation of age and conditions of entry have rendered possible effective internal organisation.

" (d) There has been developed a reasonable system of examinations, which afford a test of ordinary school work, to which the whole of the appropriate forms are submitted, and not merely selected pupils.

" (e) Of great importance has been the development of sixth form work, aided by the Advanced Course Regulations. This is of value not only to the relatively few pupils who take part in it, but generally because of its reactions on the whole school, staff and pupils alike.

" (f) Most essential of all has been the growth of a body of teachers, better educated, more generally interested in their work, and—though much remains to be done in this respect—with fuller opportunities for learning the technique of their profession."

BOOKS FOR REFERENCE

Archer: *Secondary Education*. (Cambridge University Press.)

Report on Free Places, 1918. (British Association, Burlington House.)

Recent Development of Secondary Schools. (Board of Education Pamphlet, No. 50, 1927.)

Report of Consultative Committee on the Education of the Adolescent, 1926.

CHAPTER IV

TECHNICAL AND FURTHER EDUCATION

IT is impossible to give more than a bare outline of the multiform development of this side of national education, and an imperfect sketch of the present position. The movement has had two sides to it, and these have intermingled, though they are still distinguishable. From the start it has represented a desire to give some form of education, or the opportunity of continued education, to the working classes. But it has also been an attempt to give technical instruction in arts and crafts, and so to produce the skilled operatives who will promote national efficiency, and enable us to hold our own in the field of international trade.

As early as 1760 a Scotch Professor, Anderson, of Glasgow, was holding evening classes for working men, and he left a small fortune, used to establish a chair of physics, of which Birkbeck was the first occupant. Carrying on the work in Anderson's spirit, Birkbeck gathered round him at Anderson's Institution as many as 500 working-class students. In 1823 the mechanics, as they were called, went off and founded an institution of their own, which became the parent of similar Mechanics' Institutes all over the country. By 1850 there were 600 of them. But they subordinated too often their educational work to the demands for recreation, changed their membership, and found no future in the educational system. But Anderson's old Institution survived, and in process of time has become part of the Glasgow and West of Scotland Technical College.

The nineteenth century was a period during the greater part of which little was done. Success in industry had come easily to this country, favoured, as it was, by nature and fortune: it was assumed that it was due to innate natural superiority. The success of the great Exhibition of 1851 enabled £200,000 to be set apart for science, and caused the Science and Art Department to be set up. Its purpose was to promote general education in science in order to produce men of adaptable intelligence, but specific instruction in particular industries was left to the industries themselves. Meantime, apprenticeship was fast decaying, Germany was applying scientific research to industry, and developing a great system of technical instruction. The United States were beginning to imitate Germany. None too soon, a Royal Commission was appointed, and sat from 1880 to 1884. Its work marks the turning-point in the history of technical instruction in this country, for it roused the country to the need for better secondary education as the foundation of industrial success, and for first-class technical instruction built up on that basis. It certainly produced the Technical Instruction Act of 1889, which empowered local authorities to raise a penny rate for the maintenance of Technical Schools, and it may not unfairly be regarded as the inspirer of the Bryce Commission on Secondary Education and of the Education Act of 1902.

Since then the field has been occupied in a great variety of ways, for the needs are manifold. There are the students who have left the elementary schools, and want to go further, those who have had a secondary education and want to go further, those who have been at technical classes, and want to study at a University, those who have been at a University and want to specialise and to conduct research. There are now available the Universities and University Colleges which, particularly in the case of the newer Universities, provide technological instruction to the highest level, while at Oxford and Cambridge in the last fifty years scientific research has been carried to the highest degree. There are also University Departments of Agriculture, and agricultural colleges and schools which lie outside the province of the Board of Education. Organised under the general control of the Board are very many categories of instruction : (1) Day continuation schools or courses; (2) evening schools; (3) full-time " technical instruction courses," which must include science, and be post-secondary in standard and organisation; (4) courses of advanced instruction in arts, also post-secondary in character; (5) " day technical classes " either of advanced standard, or post-elementary for pupils under sixteen; (6) junior technical schools; (7) schools of nautical training; (8) schools of art; and (9) day art classes.

The faults of the system as a system are that it has grown up in a sporadic and haphazard manner, but, at any rate, it is very flexible, and each part of it has grown to meet a need. As a result, the relations between instruction and industry itself are not close enough, and too frequently there are gaps of one, two, or more years between the close of elementary education and the beginning of technical instruction. Too much of the work has to be done in the evening, when students are tired by other occupations. The technical school is too much cut off from the elementary school which precedes it, for they are controlled by different departments of the Board, and by different administrative bodies in their localities : it is cut off again from the University institutions, which should naturally follow in the case of the best students. There is, therefore, still much to be done to create a more effective organisation, much, too, to create better buildings. For since evening work is alone possible in a very great number of instances, the classes must be held in the centre of cities, and at present many of the buildings in which they are held are unsuitable, cramped, or obsolete.

At all times evening schools of one sort or another have played a large part in further education. They have been for pupils of all ages, and, until general elementary education was organised, frequently provided the only available means of instruction. They had their origin in private benevolence, or the corporate activities of religious bodies, and they always tended to fail, because of the difficulty of obtaining regular financial support, and because there was no foundation of elementary and secondary education on which to build. The movement has had its prophets, and Owen, Maurice, Kingsley, and Ruskin all deserve their place of honour for what they have done for this side of working men's education. To-day, with the coming-in of a full system of State education, the position is materially altered. Evening classes under the Education Act of 1902 have become a definite part of the provision for higher education, and apart from this, there has grown up a large and promising organisation for adult working-class education, through the combined efforts of the Workers' Educational Association and the University Technical Classes Committees. In these classes the study is continuous, and lasts for two years : the method followed is that of lecture and discussion. The lecturer gets to know his students, and reading and essay-writing are expected. The classes are organised by the local branches of the Association, and the University Committees provide the teachers.

The extent of the field which is covered on this side of national education may be realised by the quotation of a few figures from the Board of Education Survey of Technical and Further Education, issued in 1926. Of individual students in evening schools and classes there were in 1924: in "colleges" 103,500 boys and men, 38,814 girls and women, and in other evening

2*

schools, 251,155 boys and men, 243,360 girls and women, making a grand total of 636,829 students of both sexes and all ages. There were 23,416 in day continuation schools, 11,988 in junior technical schools, 12,233 in day technical classes, 4,127 in courses of advanced instruction in art, 49,939 art students of one kind and another, and 1,529 boys receiving nautical training. About 3,000 teachers give the whole of their time to this type of work.

Very various, of course, are the motives among the students who attend these courses; the ambitions of some are humble, of others far-reaching. It requires tenacity of purpose if a student is to go far. But not a few have gone very far, and risen to positions of high responsibility, and it is due to the work of these classes that there is not in this country that deep division between the higher and the lower ranks of industry which characterises some countries. The classes themselves are never likely to be uniform in quality, but that level of attainment is bound to rise steadily as the secondary and other post-elementary schools increase, and become more efficient. The raw material should become better, and the teachers better qualified to make use of it. Already, to quote the pamphlet of the Board, " within the limits permitted to them the schools have wider aims, and with larger opportunities and better prepared students will more completely succeed as places of higher education. The responsible teachers at the present time claim it as their province to develop the intellectual powers of the students, to widen their horizons, to kindle their imaginations, to help them to find legitimate satisfaction in the exercise of their callings, and, in general, to guide them along the way of good citizenship."

Books for Reference

Survey of Technical and Further Education. (Board of Education pamphlet 49, 1926.)

Board of Education Annual Report, 1924-25.

Report of Committee on Education and Industry. First part 1926.

Draper : *University Extension.* (Cambridge University Press, 1923.)

Mansbridge : *An Adventure in Working-class Education.* (Longmans, Green and Co., 1920.)

Martin : *The Adult School Movement.* (National Adult School Union, 1924.)

Millis : *Technical Education.* (Edward Arnold, 1925.)

CHAPTER V

A GAP AND SOME LOOSE ENDS

It would not be fair to the unprofessional reader to leave him after this rapid survey of our educational system with the impression that all is well in organisation and quantity, and that all that is now necessary is an improvement in quality. On the contrary, it is to be hoped that we are approaching a reorganisation which will amount to a revolution, and a great extension of the duration of school life for large numbers of the adolescent. The organisation of the Board of Education itself into Elementary, Secondary, and Technical Departments is an indication of the wrongness of the lines on which we have been thinking. The basis of that division is not educational or psychological : it is merely historical in origin, and largely based on social distinctions. Elementary education retains its pupils to the age of fourteen, and thereby occupies three, or at least two, of the years which in the case of the normal child should go to secondary education. Those responsible for it have been forced to make uneasy and incomplete efforts to provide something like a secondary education, though under another name, for this period of overlap. Secondary schools were awkwardly linked on to elementary, for in origin there was a social distinction, and it was supposed that they provided for different classes. Secondary and elementary schools were for long, and to a large extent are, two separate worlds, and when pupils were first transferred from the latter to the former, they were transferred much too late. A large part of technical education is secondary education, or at any rate post-elementary :

44

many of the old technical classes and science schools have as a matter of history developed into normal secondary schools. There are, for instance, 202,202 students in evening schools who are under sixteen : there must be well over 10,000 students of the same age in the art schools : similar statements may be made about all the forms of instruction which fall within the survey of the Technical Department of the Board. The natural deductions have been made from these facts by the Consultative Committee of the Board of Education, which has just issued a report on "The Education of the Adolescent," known from its Chairman as the Hadow Report. That report recommends that at the beginning of the school year, 1932, the school leaving age should be raised to fifteen, and the necessary legislative and administrative steps taken to make this effective. It calls for a complete reorganisation of the schools, and demands that every normal child should pass about the age of eleven to a new type of school with curricula varied to meet the many aptitudes of the children and the needs of the varying localities. This means that elementary education is a stage through which all pass, but which stops at the age of eleven. After that, begins the secondary stage, which may extend to eighteen. But the Consultative Committee propose more than one type of school. A curriculum of the literary and scientific type is to be the feature of grammar schools, but other secondary schools with a four-year course, and a practical or material basis, are to be known as Modern Schools.

Some such reorganisation is clearly necessary if we are to deal with what at the head of this chapter has been called the gap—that is, the very large number of children who pass out of the region, not only of day-school instruction, but of all instruction and discipline whatever, at the age of fourteen. It is no exaggeration to say that by neglect of these children a large part of the effort and money devoted to the task of elementary education is consigned to waste. The children themselves are driven into temporary and blind-alley occupations, forget what they have been taught, and lose good habits. The Reports of the Poor Law Commission twenty years ago brought out the fact quite clearly that the unemployed tend largely to be young, and the unemployable not old.

Those who wish to make a close examination of the figures involved in the full consideration of this problem will find them in the Report of the Consultative Committee, or in "The Next Step in National Education," a private report on the same important subject. It appears that 348,000 children of the age fourteen to fifteen are outside the national system altogether, and 565,000 of the age fifteen to sixteen. Allowing for the fact that in any one year about 45,000 pupils may be found in the schools that are independent of the national system, that still leaves 303,000 and 520,000 as the number who have slipped through the meshes. That is a very large number when it is remembered that the total estimated population in any one year is very slightly above 700,000.

The chief attempt which has been made legislatively to deal with this problem was that of Mr. Fisher in the Act of 1918, which would have eventually required every adolescent, who was not at school till sixteen, to attend a part-time school for 320 hours a year (four hours on each of two days a week) till 18. A start was made with this scheme in London and elsewhere, but the compulsory schools perished in the campaign for economy. They had, however, brought into relief the difficulties of working them, and particularly perhaps the fact that it is not practical policy to impose the obligation on part of the community and not on the whole. If one Authority imposes it, and the next-door Authorities do not, difficulties at once arise. Compulsion was abolished in London in 1922, and the schools are continued on a voluntary basis. It is satisfactory to know that even so some 12,000 pupils are in attendance.

The scheme was ambitious, based on insufficient experience, and in the nature of a compromise. It is more worth while to consider what attempts have been made from the side of elementary education to provide for their senior pupils. It has been noticed already that the higher grade schools and schools of science were absorbed into secondary education, but this, of course, left the main problem untouched. Certain head teachers began to experiment with their curriculum and to give special teaching to their top standards to suit the commerce or industry of their localities, and it was found that children left other schools in order to secure the benefit of this instruction. So arose the idea of central schools : the term originally meant that selected pupils from a number of schools were sent to a school which was geographically central, but it now means a particular type of post-primary education. Pupils in London are selected at the age of eleven, either by examination or by record, and they follow a four-year course on secondary lines : the curriculum has a practical trend, but it is not devoted to technical training for any particular industry or business. But the system is being tried out in many areas, and at Manchester, where there are now nineteen schools, Mr. Spurley Hey reports that while these schools admit pupils from the same areas and on the same examination as the secondary schools, yet the school life is shorter, classes are larger, the cost is cheaper, and the pupils more commonly enter upon industrial occupations. Non-selective central schools are being tried in Surrey, but owing to the difference of attainments of those who enter have to be worked in each case as virtually two schools.

Elsewhere the same problem is dealt with from

within the elementary schools themselves. Leicester maintains two types of elementary schools for children over eleven, for those who are fit for secondary education but cannot find places, and for those who have a practical rather than an academic bent. Nottingham, by examination, finds out which at eleven years of age are the abler children, and proposes to send 10 per cent. to secondary schools, 30 to 40 per cent. to central schools, and the remainder to special elementary schools with a wider curriculum. Carlisle organises its education in such a way that all pupils at the age of eleven go either to secondary schools or to district senior schools. In all these cases it is obvious that the more progressive authorities feel that elementary education proper ends at eleven, and that a new organisation is then necessary. Experience goes to show that the next step should be not to endeavour to float a large scheme of part-time education, but to secure a firm hold on all the children from the age of eleven to fifteen, and to make this definitely a course of secondary education, the characteristics of which shall be flexibility and variety.

A thorough-going reorganisation of the Board of Education's constitution will be necessary, and equally a rearrangement of the Local Education Authorities. The sphere of authority of a local authority in education should be large, for homogeneous communities are widespread, and people to-day sleep and have their homes at considerable distances from their work. Above all there should be a single authority within an area for all forms of education, and the anomaly at present surviving, that there are 318 authorities for elementary education, and 145 for higher education, should be swept away, for no truly national and co-ordinated system can be made until this occurs.

Another survival which hampers progress is the dualism in elementary education of the "provided" and "non-provided" schools. As has been said, this has been left alone, and the denominations are still charged with the maintenance of fabrics and the selection of teachers, because attempts to alter this awaken at once the fire of religious controversy. To many it seems that this controversy has no substance, and that the denominations would serve their own purposes better if they combined to secure in every area an agreed syllabus of Christian instruction under a conscience clause for teachers and taught, and devoted the effort and expenditure, which they now devote to the task of maintaining their schools, to the reform and expansion of their Sunday Schools, where the denominational teaching could most properly be given. The problem of how to secure adequate religious instruction within the rapidly growing sphere of secondary education is one which is really of more vital importance, but the old embers still smoulder and engage the attention of denominationalists, and they are not awake to the greater danger, that in a very few years from now all children over the age of eleven will be in courses of secondary education which so far offer little scope for religious teaching of any sort. There is, however, increasing goodwill, and a general, almost universal, desire that the principles of Christianity shall be adequately taught. It is much to be hoped that the denominations will bury old animosities and combine to bring it about that the coming system of national education shall be effectively Christian.

[NOTE.—The magnitude of the problem can be estimated from a few figures. In 1924-25 there were 11,698 voluntary schools, with 15,461 departments, and 1,759,998 children; 9,038 Council schools, with 15,592 departments, and 3,180,463 children. The number of Council schools tends to increase at about the rate of 150 a year, and of voluntary schools to decrease at the rate of 120 a year.]

BOOKS FOR REFERENCE

Report of Consultative Committee on Education of the Adolescent, 1926.

The Next Step in Education. (University of London Press, 1927.)

Tawney : *Secondary Education for All.* (Allen and Unwin, 1922.)

Spurley Hey : *The Central School.* (Manchester Co-operative Society, 1924.)

Wray and Ferguson : *Day Continuation School at Work.* (Longmans, 1926.)

Birchington : *Education in Leicestershire since the War.* (1925.)

CHAPTER VI

THE UNIVERSITIES

ABOVE the great system of secondary and technical
education lies the sphere of the Universities and
University Colleges, self-governing and independent,
though not entirely unaided by the State. In the last
hundred years Oxford and Cambridge have been
several times reformed, and all the others have been
born—of many of them it can be said that they were
begotten in the nineteenth century and born in the
twentieth. The two oldest Universities, which were for
so long a period of English history the only Universities, are still expensive and residential, but by the
aid of scholarships and grants of many kinds they are
in effect open to, and used by, all classes of the community. They have discarded all tests, even for
theological degrees. They are governed by a council of
residents, with a final right of veto reserved for the
whole body of masters, both resident and non-resident.
In spite of the jests that this only means that country
parsons are privileged at will to block reform and
change, it remains true that Oxford has admitted
women to degrees, and Nonconformists to theological
degrees, and has abolished compulsory Greek. Neither
fellowships nor scholarships are any longer abused,
and the compromise between the professorial and
tutorial system has worked singularly well in practice.
The professors in a real measure control policy and
research, and have a very dominant position in the
natural sciences. The tutors lecture publicly, and not
to their own pupils only, while with these pupils they
have established a tradition of cordial relationship
which is one of the happiest features of the old

Universities. Both Universities have done much for research, especially of late years, in all branches of human knowledge, and those who regard them as in the main cultivators of the obsolete and the traditional are very wide of the mark. At no period of their history have they been in closer touch with the full stream of the national life, and their primacy is not likely to be shaken in the least by the growth of newer rivals.

University College, London, was founded as long ago as 1827 as the nucleus of a University from which theology was to be excluded. King's College was the answer of the religious to the secularists, and it began its career in the following year. Eight years later a charter was granted to the new University of London, which was to consist of the two already existing colleges and any other of University rank that should be founded. Owens College, Manchester, did not follow till 1851. Both in the south and in the north these new institutions opened higher education to those who refused religious tests: they recognised from the start the value of applied science, and they were homes of learning possible for the poor.

The fortune of development prevented London from being the teaching University which it had set out to be, though University College and King's College continued their full University work; in 1858 it took the unhappy step of awarding its degrees solely on examination. This has only been reversed in quite recent years, and London University, after two Royal Commissions, remains a very complicated body. It is organised by faculties, and it embraces a variety of institutions as schools in these faculties, the two original University Colleges, Bedford and Holloway, the women's colleges, the medical schools of the hospitals, the East London College, the Imperial College of Science and Technology, the Royal College of Science, the School of Mines, the City and Guilds

Colleges, the South-Eastern Agricultural College, and the London School of Economics. It has, moreover, six schools in the faculty of theology. It still retains a large number of external as well as internal students, and has at last found the definite home which it has long wanted, in the site behind the British Museum.

In the North, Durham University began as long ago as 1831, and was meant to be a group of residential colleges after the ancient model. In 1882 it absorbed the Newcastle Medical School, and later the Armstrong College of Science, so that it combines two atmospheres, the cathedral city with the industrial, the old with the new.

Owens College, Manchester, was the first of a vigorous progeny. Founded in 1851, and passing through a delicate infancy, it then developed steadily, and Yorkshire College was founded in 1874 in imitation of it. These two were combined into the Victoria University in 1880, which was to contain also a college at Liverpool, as soon as it could be erected. University College, Liverpool, came into being in the following year. In 1870, Mason College had been founded in Birmingham with a strong, practical, and utilitarian bent, which it lost only slowly, but it had the distinction of becoming the first University confined to one provincial city, and in 1900 took rank as the University of Birmingham. Almost immediately Victoria University defederalised itself, for the constitution had proved itself in practice very inconvenient, and all the colleges had grown. In 1903, therefore, Manchester, Leeds, and Liverpool took rank with Birmingham, and from similar origins Sheffield followed in 1905, and Bristol in 1909. Similar movements which will convert provincial University Colleges into Universities are in progress elsewhere.

These modern Universities were meant to bring intellectual life into the daily work of the modern world, to spread humanism, and to develop the application of science to industry. They have been greatly successful on the whole. They have opened the highest education to many who were entirely shut off, and have brought it to the doors of all large centres of population. They have not neglected the older subjects of culture, while they have widely extended the range of subjects, largely technological, which are proper to University work. They have knit together English society, for, while the remoteness and aloofness of Oxford and Cambridge had put the professions out of sympathy with industry and commerce, the new Universities created a new sympathy, and at the same time reacted on the old, so that these, too, learned to meet the new needs. Their weakest point is their lack of true corporate life, but this, too, is being met by the creation of Halls of Residence, and it may well come about in this century that a morale and a corporate spirit will be engendered which will enable these Universities to stand comparison with any of the old.

BOOKS FOR REFERENCE

Royal Commission on Oxford and Cambridge Universities. 2 vols. 1922.

Ellis : *The Poor Student and the University*. (Labour Publishing Co.) 1927.

Yearbook of the Universities of the Empire. (Bell and Sons.)

CHAPTER VII

THE EDUCATION OF GIRLS AND WOMEN

THE history of the movement by which women claimed, and made good, their right to an equal education with that of men, is one of great interest, but it is too long for a handbook. Those who would understand its spirit rightly should read the biographies of the women who were the pioneers, for the success which was gained was the personal achievement of a few great women of the middle class. Here can be set down only a few of the important events, and a brief statement of the position as it stands to-day.

It has been on the whole a movement led by women for women, though Queen's College, in date (1847) the first college for women, and really a lecturing agency and offshoot of King's College, was the creation of Maurice. In 1869 Bedford College, now a constituent college of London University, followed, and Miss Emily Davies founded at Hitchin her college for women, which has since developed into Girton. In 1875 Miss Clough became the first Principal of Newnham. The attack on Oxford developed a little later, but Somerville College and Lady Margaret Hall were established by 1879.

They were tolerated by some, derided by many, and the object of the boundless enthusiasm of a few. London University, after long controversy, admitted women to its degrees in 1878, Victoria University in 1880, the Scotch Universities in 1892; in Wales, from the foundation of the . University, men and women were equal. It was not till after the war that

Oxford granted the same privilege, and Cambridge has not done so yet.

On the whole, in accordance with the general English tradition, the inspiration for women's education has come from the Universities, and thence descended to the schools. Those who care to inquire into the condition of girls' education in the early part of the nineteenth century will find store of very amusing reading, but they will be very sorry for the girls who had to endure it. Whether the schools were expensive (and some were very expensive) or cheap, they seem to have been uniformly bad: repression, superficiality, and convention were their features. The Schools Enquiry Commission in 1868 summed up the complaints which were made against them as: "Want of thoroughness and foundation; slovenliness and showy superficiality; inattention to rudiments; undue time given to accomplishments, and those not taught intelligently, or in any scientific manner; want of organisation." It is a sufficiently damning indictment. In 1857 Miss Beale was an assistant-mistress at the School for Clergymen's Daughters, and was required to teach, week by week, Scripture, arithmetic, mathematics, ancient and modern history, geography, English, French, German, Latin, and Italian. Further comment is needless.

In the following year Miss Beale was appointed to Cheltenham College, and found her life's work. She created a great model, at once a day-school and a boarding-school with a range covering the whole field of elementary and secondary education. Some years later Miss Buss handed her flourishing school over to a trust, and it became the North London Collegiate School, the model of the high schools. In 1872 the Girls' Public Day School Company was founded, and the movement became committed to the ideal of day-schools in towns and cities. It was largely the result of private effort, and means were lacking to create

boarding-schools of the type then becoming common
for boys.

The Schools Inquiry Commission only considered
girls' schools because they did not happen to be excluded by its terms of reference, but its report in
1868 is a great landmark. It led to the Endowed
Schools Act of 1869, which made possible the foundation of girls' schools out of the surplus funds of the
boys' schools, where these existed, and by the end of
the nineteenth century there were in existence upwards
of 80 endowed schools for girls. On the whole,
the dominant tradition of the day-school has been
maintained, but in the last twenty-five years public
boarding-schools have been founded in fair numbers,
and have succeeded; it is probable that a considerable future lies before them.

Inspiring as this movement had been, it had owed
very little to the helping hand of the State, which did
not take part until the Education Act of 1902 made
it possible for Local Education Authorities to do their
duty by the secondary education of girls in their areas.
What has happened since then can be summed up in
a few telling statistics. In 1902 there were on the
Board's list 99 girls' schools; in 1925 there were 403;
in the same period 184 co-educational schools had
grown to 361. The 33,159 pupils had increased to
173,273, and had more than quintupled themselves.

It is impossible for growth to take place as rapidly
as this without developing strains in the fabric, and
those responsible for the schools are finding it very
hard to bring this great mass of new material
through the full course of secondary education without imposing upon them undue strain. Hitherto, and
quite rightly, the leaders of the movement for women's
education have been concerned to demonstrate the
equality of men and women, boys and girls, and they
have therefore tended to insist on following an
identical course of instruction. There are many who

think that, so far as secondary education is concerned, for the great mass of girls this has become an illogical procedure, and they look anxiously for the coming of some personality strong enough to shape the new education into a form which will suit the needs of girls as such, the future wives and mothers of the men of the nation.

But women have already made considerable contribution to the general good of education. More than men they have realised the value of training, and devoted attention to method and the art of exposition. It is to be noted that the two most valuable recent developments on this side of education have both come from women, working out theories in practice, from Madame Montessori, who is exercising a great influence on the training of the early years of childhood in many nations, and from Miss Mason, whose methods inspire a good many primary and private secondary schools in this country, and are gaining ground.

Co-education offers a vexed field of discussion into which there is not space to enter fully. There are 361 co-educational schools known to the Board, and there are a few others. Most of these are co-educational simply for reasons of economy: the few are the creation of those who believe intensely that the sexes should throughout be educated together. There is, however, no doubt that the bulk of teachers, both men and women, like the mass of the nation, believe that while boys and girls are fitly educated together in the earliest years, and should meet again at the University, the intervening years are better spent apart in the interest of both sexes alike.

BOOKS FOR REFERENCE

Archer: *Reform of Female Education*. (Chap. ix. of *Secondary Education*. Cambridge University Press.)

Burstall: *English High Schools for Girls* (Longmans). *Lives of Miss Clough, Miss Buss, and Miss Beale*. (Now out of print.)

Consultative Committee's Report on Differentiation of Curriculum for Boys and Girls.

Woods: *Co-education*. (Sidgwick and Jackson, 1919.)

CHAPTER VIII

THE ADMINISTRATORS OF THE SYSTEM

A. THE BOARD OF EDUCATION

IN 1829 a Committee of the Privy Council was charged with the duty of superintending the application of any expenditure which might be approved for the purpose of assisting public education. By 1856 this grew into an Education Department, which was still in theory a Committee of Council. Its powers were increased in 1870 when the Education Act gave it power to extend and to improve elementary education, and its sphere of influence continued to extend. So did that of the Science and Art Department, and such was the overlapping and interpenetration of the two authorities that all saw that a single central authority was necessary. In 1899 accordingly the two Departments were constituted into a Board charged with the care of education in England and Wales. It has a President, who has a seat in Parliament, and changes when Governments change: but as a Board it never meets, though it has a definite membership and could meet if it were desired.

There was much anxious consideration in those days, for it was feared that to place all education under a Government Department would deaden it until it became mechanical, that it would fall under the influence of party politics, and that the transient politicians who were at the head of the Department would inevitably concede power to the permanent officials. Various schemes for the setting up of an educational council were proposed, discussed, and in the end rejected. Probably this was wise. The system has not worked at all badly, and the evil consequences have not made themselves very apparent. The Board have made no attempt to grasp the whole of power, and the freedom which they have left to secondary schools has reacted with good effect on elementary education. It is improbable that better results would have followed if such bodies as the Teachers' Registration Council or the Consultative Committee had been in charge of national educational policy. It has become increasingly clear that it is the business of teachers to teach and to mind their schools, and of trained specialists to administer. For the educational machine has become very complicated, as it has developed, and it is the work of a lifelong apprenticeship to learn to manage that important side of the system that consists of organisation and finance.

In the years following its institution the Board was organised into the three departments of Elementary, Secondary, and Technical, and concentrated in Whitehall : of these it still consists. Reasons have been stated in a previous chapter for the belief that this organisation no longer meets present facts. The work of organising the new office and adjusting its operations to the activities of the new Local Education Authorities, when they came, was performed with distinction by Sir Robert Morant, who was Permanent Secretary from 1903 to 1911.

Since the Education Act of 1918, and the consolidation of the law relating to education in the Act of 1921, the Board has come to hold itself to be in partnership with the Local Authorities for the promotion of a common task, with which it endeavours not to interfere too much in detail, and leaves to the other side the larger measure of initiative. It trusts to the local bodies to be the best judges of local needs, and to local enthusiasm to carry through the necessary tasks. Hence, it has of late years called for schemes of development to be framed by the varying localities for themselves, and has abolished the system of particular grants, establishing in their place the minimum percentage grant in aid of the total local expenditure. It has so far as possible frankly dispensed with detailed codes of regulations, and trusts to the spirit of co-operation and the awakened keenness of all members of the educational service. Nothing, for instance, could be wider or less hampering than the following regulation, which comes from the Regulations of 1926: "Secular instruction in a school or centre must be in accordance with a suitable curriculum and syllabus framed with due regard to the organisation and circumstances of the school or schools concerned."

The Board is not supreme over the whole of national education. It has no authority over Universities or University Colleges. Save under the Endowed Schools Act or Charitable Trusts Act, it has no authority over endowed schools which do not receive grants of public money, none over schools conducted for private profit, of which there are very many, and none over the comparatively few schools under other Government Departments. It has nothing directly to do with the payment, appointment, or dismissal of teachers, the choice of textbooks, or the details of the curriculum.

It is a friendly critic, adviser, and helper, spurring on the backward authority, and sometimes of late, under the pressure of public economy, holding back the eager. It has to count the cost, for while it does not order schools to be built, it contributes largely to the necessary expenditure: it must take long views. It is easy for the reformer to say that at least twenty in every thousand of the population should be at secondary schools, but this means in effect doubling the number of schools and doubling the supply of teachers: both problems very much concern the Board. It is responsible for the efficiency of schools, and for seeing that the nation receives value for its money; here again the Board endeavours not to apply stereotyped standards, but within the necessarily complicated organisation which it maintains, to leave room for flexibility and experiment. Efficiency in particular it is impossible to define, for education is qualitative, not quantitative : Browning has pointed out that the man who misses a million may for all that produce a far higher result than the man who is content with a hundred. But the latter could, on a narrow definition, be efficient, and the former not. The Board declares that every school must be kept on a satisfactory level of efficiency, but all that it can do is to help to bring each group of schools up to the level of the next above. The methods which it can employ are effective, for it has in its hands the use of regulations, the visits of criticism and advice paid by inspectors, the training of a large part of the teaching profession, and all that can be done by the distribution of information.

Certain organisations, subordinate to, or connected with the Board, deserve to be mentioned, for they have all played their part in the development of English education. (1) The Consultative Committee, which now consists of twenty-one members, appointed by the President for a term of six years. In its origin it was all that came out of the plan for a governing council for education, propounded, and strongly advocated, at the end of last century. But it has justified its existence by producing thirteen important reports, not the least valuable of which have been the two recent ones on differentiation between the sexes, and on the education of the adolescent. It is still disputed whether it has a statutory power to offer advice or merely to be consulted at the discretion of the Board; it is a theoretic difficulty which offers little difficulty in practice. (2) The Teachers' Registration Council, which has had a troubled history, like the register which it keeps. It was established in 1912, reconstituted in 1926, and is now independent of the Board. Registered teachers, divided into 23 groups, elect its members. It is charged with the duty of keeping a register of teachers, and ultimately of enforcing training. In October, 1926, it had 74,000 teachers on the register, of whom 45,000 were elementary, 19,000 secondary, 8,000 specialist, 400 University, and 2,000 private. As there must be considerably more than 200,000 teachers altogether, this is not an altogether impressive result of fifteen years' work, and to many its practical good is not apparent. (3) The Secondary Schools Examinations Council, consisting of members who are partly representative and partly nominated by the President. It is charged with the duty of helping in the organisation and co-ordination of school examinations. It is, in the main, responsible for the system of the First and Second Examinations in the secondary schools, and it has carried out two sets of "investigations" of these examinations as conducted by the eight examining authorities, which have been valuable, because they have brought school and University teachers, inspectors, and administrators together in a common task. (4) The Juvenile Organisations Committee, a product of the war, which was meant to stimulate voluntary effort to supplement State education. It is understood that this now languishes through lack of funds. (5) The Office of Special Inquiries and Reports, inspired in its inception in 1894 by Sir Michael Sadler. It has produced 28 volumes of reports. (6) Special Committees: (a) those known as the Prime Minister's Committees, which after the war reported on English, Natural Science, Modern Languages, and Classics—a valuable series of reports, which expressed the mind and experience of one generation on the greater part of the subjects of secondary education; (b) those presided over by Viscount Burnham, which have successfully dealt with the problems of the pay and the pensions of teachers, and are known as Burnham Committees. (7) Educational Pamphlets and Circulars of the Board, which from time to time summarise the history and present position of some portion of the educational system, or of some subject of the curriculum, and are frequently documents of great educational value.

B. The Inspectorate

This is so important a part of the educational machinery maintained by the Board that it requires separate treatment. It was last organised in 1904-05 into five groups for five main branches: (1) elementary, (2) secondary, (3) technical, (4) training of teachers, and (5) art. The first three groups have each a chief inspector, one of whom is the senior for control and co-ordination. There is a Chief Woman Inspector, nine Division Inspectors, and below these District and Assistant Inspectors. There are some who hold strongly that inspectors should always be drawn from the ranks of those who have actually taught in schools. A certain number undoubtedly should be so chosen, but it is probably wiser to say that they should be appointed wherever the right personality is found and whatever the previous training, for they need personality, tact, sympathy, and some measure of statesmanship. They are sent out not to spy and to restrict freedom and experiment, but to help good work wherever they see it, and by criticism and advice to improve bad work. They carry ideas from one school to another, and they carry the ideas of the schools back to the Board. They prevent undue pressure on schools, particularly the pressure of political and social propaganda. In two words, their function is protective and constructive, and they have been, so far as any one body of men can claim the honour, the main agents of the undoubted advance which has been made in education in the last twenty-five years.

3

In elementary schools inspection began as long ago as 1839, but it became a formidable system when in 1862 payment by results was instituted, and he who should have been the friendly inspector became the dreaded examiner. He had to examine all the children in the elements, and two-thirds of the grant depended on the result. The system was bad for teachers and taught, but when it was abolished the pendulum swung too far the other way, as usually happens; in 1901, for instance, the inspector was confined to criticism and advice, and it was held that the teacher was the only proper examiner. Now things are moving to a more sensible compromise. Inspectors freely question elementary pupils, and inspect their work, but it has been well pointed out that the new spirit is shown by the fact that the Board no longer issues Instructions to Inspectors, but Suggestions to Teachers. It is to be noted also that examination is coming back again into the elementary schools in the shape of tests for scholarships and free places. There were 134,177 free places in 1925-26.

The inspection of secondary schools naturally did not begin until after 1902. It was made a condition, if a school was to receive grant, but it was also offered free to schools which were not in receipt of grant, and after 1906 to such as wished to be styled " efficient." There are very few schools which have not undergone, to their own great profit, inspection by the Board, for the Board's secondary inspectors by long practice have become specialists, and no private agency or University can provide men and women of equal sagacity and experience. A " full " inspection means that a team of inspectors spend the greater part of a week within a school, and observe the curriculum, the teaching, the buildings, the finance, and the whole life of the place; they then confer with the governing body, and subsequently issue a report. It is an exhausting process for those concerned, and inspection has been freely attacked, and sometimes unreasonably, for, after all, the public has a right to know that its money is being properly expended, and how else or more helpfully could this knowledge be gained? However, the Board's are not the only inspectors: the local authorities sometimes maintain them, too, and there has in the past been something in the complaint that schools were too much inspected, too harassed and interrupted, and too liable to be exposed to the " fads " of successive inspectors. The other line of attack, that inspection makes for a rigid uniformity, and the suppression of initiative and experiment, is simply without foundation: the opposite is rather true. And even the outcry against the frequency and the interrupting character of the Board's inspections must in honesty be tempered by the reflection that a school is exposed to full inspection only once in ten years.

C. The Local Education Authorities

It has been observed already that there are 318 authorities for elementary education, and 145 for higher education, and that this arrangement, which cannot last beyond the next reorganisation of our national system, greatly complicates the vitally important work of co-ordinating elementary with secondary education in all its forms. They are of very varying sizes, for at one end of the 318 may be found Rutland, with a population of 18,368, and at the other Lancashire, with a population of 1,746,139, and London, with 4,483,249, in itself as big as a small nation. The County Boroughs range from Canterbury, with 23,738, to Birmingham, with 919,438. Strange as it may seem, even London for all its size is not big enough, for it has very many outside its borders who properly belong to it, and it is debarred from doing many things if its neighbours do not follow suit.

Each authority has an Education Committee, the members of which are elected by popular vote, though they can by co-optation add to their numbers experts and advisers. They may be, and are, elected for quite other non-educational qualifications. But this system has undoubtedly worked better than the old School Boards, which were elected specifically for educational work, and in which denominational feeling was apt to run riot. Close upon 10,000 men and women are giving their time and money to this valuable educational service, and perhaps do not receive the full measure of honour which is their due. They are assisted by permanent officials, who since 1902 have become a necessity. All the larger authorities have a Chief Education Officer with a trained staff, a Director of Education, or a Secretary for Education —in the smaller boroughs these duties are often part of the work of the Town Clerk. This permanent staff of the local authorities has a great field of public service in front of it in organisation and finance. But there are some who feel—indeed it is a universal feeling in the schools—that there is a danger that some of these officials may unwisely interfere too much with that freedom and initiative which the Board of Education has been careful to safeguard, and done much to promote, in the schools themselves.

Those who would know how many-sided is the work which a Local Education Authority has to conduct could not do better than study such a book as *The London Education Service,* which has been prepared for the London County Council largely for the service of the thousands of visitors who come each year to study what is being done. It is, of course, far the largest of our Authorities, but that enables the reader the better to estimate the multiplicity of the task. It maintains a large administrative staff, and an Inspectorate of its own. It has within its survey 913 ordinary elementary schools, 74 central schools, 10 open-air schools, 153 schools for children in one way or another defective, 5 industrial schools, 79 secondary schools, and 5 training colleges of its own with 1,398 students in attendance. The work of medical inspection occupies 23 doctors whole time, and 70 part time, 60 dentists, and 350 school nurses. There are 250 day and evening continuation schools, and adult education is promoted through the London University and its colleges, the Workers' Educational Association, the polytechnics and settlements, and men's and women's institutes. There are four ways of circulating books, and 2,000,000 volumes in the circulation scheme alone. The Council further works in close touch with the University, aids many sides of its work, and entirely maintains one school of the University—the Day Training College. These examples, chosen at random and by no means complete, show clearly enough how great a part the local Education Authority plays in securing the well-being of London.

The partnership of the Central with the Local Authorities in the work of national education is fraught with great hope, if it continues to be animated by the spirit with which it has begun. The absence of detailed regulation secures to the local Authorities and to their schools a greater measure of freedom and of responsibility : equally it makes the Central Authority more absolute, because its discretion is unfettered. Sir Amherst Selby-Bigge rightly says, in his book, *The Board of Education,* speaking of the new regulations : " Whether they are successful will depend entirely on the way and on the spirit in which they are worked. If they are worked in the spirit of paymaster and claimant, they will make matters very difficult for both parties, especially as their form exposes their working more, and not less, to the influence of political fluctuations. If they are worked in the spirit of partnership, and a genuine acceptance on both sides of the obligations and conditions of partnership, they may contribute greatly to the consolidation of that relation."

BOOKS FOR REFERENCE

Selby-Bigge: *The Board of Education*. (Putnam, 1927.)

Board of Education Annual Reports for 1913-14, 1922-23. (The Inspectorate.)

The London Education Service. (The County Hall, London, 1927.)

Balfour: *Educational Administration*. (Clarendon Press, 1921.)

Simon: *A City Council from Within*. (Longmans, Green and Co., 1926.)

CHAPTER IX

HEALTH AND PHYSIQUE

THERE is one form of progress which is visible to the eye of even the casual observer, and that is the health and general well-being of the children at the schools. It is nearly all a progress of the last twenty years, for the feeding of schoolchildren began with the Education (Provision of Meals) Act of 1906, and medical inspection was brought in by the Education (Administrative Provisions) Act of 1907. Much educational progress is invisible, and often it is disputable; but the annual report of the Chief Medical Officer of the Board of Education always records progress, and is among the most inspiring educational documents of the year. It is odd that the nation should have waited until the twentieth century before realising that it is as important to make the child fit to receive education as to devise an education to fit the child. Fifty years ago in the elementary schools of London there were 85 children on the average to a single teacher : they were badly fed and clothed in rags. Child misery was so common that it moved Dr. Barnardo to enter upon his life's work to succour their destitution. What has been done since may be illustrated from the following passage taken from the Report of the Education Officer for London, 1926 : "The following notes on a school, which for many years was looked upon as probably the poorest in London, may be of interest. In the early days the school was a battle ground. The neighbourhood was at war with the school authorities : the children were at war with the teachers; and the parents took the side of the children. Physical violence was frequent, truancy was common. The children were sent to school wretchedly clothed and wretchedly fed : in winter, even when snow was on the ground, many boys came to school without boots and stockings. The teachers often used to buy bread at their own expense for the children." The first struggle was to make them obey rules, the next to overcome sullenness, indifference, and hostility, the next to win their goodwill. Now the next generation has arrived at the school, but the whole neighbourhood has improved. Housing is better, and wages are better. " No child is now without boots : hardly any are in torn clothes : none is in rags. There are no truants, for the children like the quietness of the school. The parents are better than the previous generation. The present generation is better than its parents. The parents trust the teachers, upholding them in any disciplinary measures they may take." In producing this happy result medical inspection and physical care, and the treatment of children as human individuals, have played the largest part.

The object of the medical service is to detect all departures from normal health, and growth, and to advise the proper remedy. This in the first place; but it seeks to go farther, to find out the causes of the defects, and to prevent them : last, its purpose is to teach, and to cause the children to practise, personal hygiene in every school. As a matter of routine every child is medically examined three times in its school life, at the ages of five, eight, and twelve, but opportunity is given both to parents and to teachers to consult the medical adviser at any time, if need arises. Every year sees an advance made, which is not surprising to those who reflect that less than the space of one generation has elapsed since neglect was total. But much further progress can still be made. The life of the child before it arrives at school requires more supervision and care, for the schools are the receivers of damaged goods, and that damage has been done in the very early years. Hygiene can be better taught, and experience is always improving the methods and adequacy of clinical study. More use can be made of open air and sunlight. But already Sir George Newman claims that there are at any rate six points in which the London school child of 1924 differs favourably from the child of 1894. (*a*) He is better clothed, and he is cleaner; (*b*) his posture and carriage are improved; (*c*) he is more intelligent and happier; (*d*) his physique is stronger; (*e*) mouth breathing has ceased to be common; (*f*) the carriage of the hands is different.

In a progressive authority such as London all the children are examined by nurses in all the schools every term : they are made to wash and keep themselves clean. This inspection enables all departures from normal health to be brought to the notice of the doctors. The children are weighed and measured, and their sight roughly tested : they are sent on, if need be, to the dentist or the opthalmologist. When the children are found to be ailing, they are dealt with by the School Care Committees, who are groups of voluntary workers attached to each school, or small group of schools. In London these committees now number one thousand : they give personal service and bring the human touch and individual care into the child's life. They choose the children who are insufficiently fed, and arrange that they shall receive proper meals until they can be properly fed at home. They visit the homes, get to know the mothers, and arrange how best the treatment advised by the doctor can be carried out; they make the appointments at the treatment centres. They give special attention to those children who for any cause are going through a bad time, and facing difficulties whether they come upon them from within or without; they advise parents as to employment, and try to obtain a suitable future for the children when they leave. There are special Care

Committees for the after-care of the blind, deaf, and defective children, and they are singularly successful. The last London report says: "Numbers of children are also sent away from London into the country to epileptic colonies, to open-air camp schools, to the ophthalmic school at Swanley, to the ear hospital at Sutton, to tuberculosis sanatoria, and to hospitals for the rheumatic. Remedial classes are also held in many schools for the benefit of children requiring more than the usual amount of physical exercises. Provision is thus made for dealing according to their physical needs with every type of child, and the help and solicitude evinced by the whole school organisation for the exceptional child has borne fruit in the much improved standard of health and physique which has been established in London."

One other reflection may be put on record. There has, in recent years, been a wonderful fall in infant mortality and a remarkable saving of child life. This has been directly due to the teaching of doctors and nurses, but its real cause lies deeper. It is that the parents of the present generation are those who have been through the reformed type of elementary education which has now so happily established itself.

BOOKS FOR REFERENCE

Annual Reports of the Chief Medical Officer of the Board of Education.

The London Education Service.

CHAPTER X

THE TEACHERS

In a book of this character least need be said about those who are most important, for every reader will have had acquaintance with schoolmaster or schoolmistress. The purpose of the book is to describe the system of organisation, supply, and control behind the fighting line, not to discuss the thoughts of those who man the trenches and bear the brunt of the battle. In spite of all the great work which the nineteenth century accomplished for education, it left the status of the teacher too low, and his salary too meagre. The elementary schoolmaster received payment of a very moderate kind, whatever his responsibilities, and the pension to which he looked forward was a mere pittance. In secondary schools it was found in 1894 that the average salary of 800 masters in some 200 schools was only slightly in excess of £100 a year : the portion of women teachers was worse. In neither case was there any pension for them to look forward to. Many of them had undertaken their life's work from a sense of vocation, and did not complain : but there were many hardships, and even tragedies, which closed lives spent in the public service, which were in truth a disgrace to a wealthy nation. Improvement began after 1902, but even in 1914 the average salary of assistant masters in secondary schools stood at £174, and of women at £126. Circumstances are now changed. In 1925 the average salary of headmasters was £763, of headmistresses £598, of assistant masters £390, and of assistant mistresses £310. What is still more important, all those who serve in the State-aided schools and classes look forward to a pension.

It is generally agreed that the quality of teachers has improved. In the case of elementary teachers, they have usually had the advantage of a much more humane and liberal education than their predecessors, and a course of professional training is a regular thing with them. In secondary schools there has been very great expansion, and for a time the war very seriously interfered with supply. There were in 1908 9,325 men and women teachers in this type of education, in the State-aided schools for which alone figures are available, and in 1925 these had grown to 19,604, 9,718 being men and 9,886 women. The percentage of graduates among the men had risen in the same period from 62 per cent. to 80, and among the women from 41 to 62. On the other hand, in the matter of training undergone before teaching, the women are superior to the men, though in both cases the proportion of the trained to the untrained steadily rises. Just over 40 per cent. of the men, and over 50 per cent. of the women have undergone some course of training. It is to be remembered that the fact that a teacher is not a graduate does not mean that he or she is inefficient, for there are many subjects in secondary education for which qualifications are required other than those of a university degree.

The benefits which have been showered upon the teaching profession in the form of assured salary-scales and pensions are not entirely without drawbacks. They mean that it is far less possible for a teacher to pass to another school once a certain seniority, and therefore expensiveness, on the salary-scale has been reached : it is far less possible to pass the gap which divides the State-aided from the independent schools. Interchange and free movement between types of schools are in themselves good, and the limitation is to be regretted. It is also a more serious thing than it was for a teacher to become unemployed in middle-life, for new appointments in the interests of economy are almost always made from those who are beginning their career. These defects are not to be lost sight of, but they weigh little in comparison with the great advantages which have been conferred.

Teachers have organised themselves into Sectional Associations, which once a year fill the papers with their discussions, and do perhaps more useful work in their committees and councils, meeting throughout the year and discussing privately questions of professional interest. Most would agree that educational conferences are too numerous, and meet too frequently : they are more in the nature of parades than councils, and their programmes are too frequently artificial. Thring first convened what became the Headmasters' Conference in 1869. It is a misunderstood body. It numbers about 150 members, the headmasters of schools which have a separate and independent Governing Body, and some regular connection with the Universities. It meets for discussion, interchange of ideas, and the settling of common action about questions where common action is desirable. It has never pretended to govern the profession or its constituent schools, or to settle the vexed question of what is or is not a Public School. In the following year, 1870, that which is the largest association was formed, the National Union of Teachers, a powerful body, something of a great trade union of the elementary teachers, which has maintained its representatives in Parliament. Others came thick and fast : the Headmistresses in 1874, the Private Schools in 1883, the Headmasters, a much more catholic body than the Conference, in 1890, the Assistant Masters, and the Preparatory Schools in 1892. There are a good many others. They have to do in the main with educational policies and professional questions, and in other associations teachers, either in common with others who are not in schools, or segregated into societies, whose members are all of one kidney, discuss the questions that concern the curriculum and the staple subjects of education. Such are the English Association, the Historical Association, the Modern Language, the Geographical, the Classical Associations, or that of the Science Masters. There are many others of smaller range and membership, for they are apt to shoot up wherever two or three enthusiasts gather together.

All that has been considered in this book ends ultimately in the teacher in his classroom, standing in the presence of those whom he teaches. That alone is of supreme and ultimate value. In two ways there has been great progress. The old aloofness of the teacher and the old hostility or indifference of the taught have disappeared. Whether it be the tutor in the University, or the secondary teacher in schools ancient or new, or the elementary teacher in city or village, it is true that the spirit of the relationship between teacher and taught has changed for the better : the teacher tries to be the friend, philosopher, and guide of his pupils. Secondly, slowly as the national system of education takes shape, there emerges a sense of unity throughout the whole teaching profession, a self-consciousness of high vocation which may be capable of great things. The profession begins to feel that in every part of it it is engaged in the national service which is most vital of all, the creation of an educated democracy such as the world has not yet seen. Unless that democracy is created, Britain will prove unequal to the burden and responsibility of her position in the world; unless it is created, there is strong probability that the country will work its own ruin. It feels, also, with growing conviction, that it alone can build that education on the basis of practical religion, since through its hands alone passes the whole youth of the nation. In face of its great work it asks in all its branches for the fullest measure of freedom, and the amplest room for initiative and experiment that can be conceded, that it may not fail in the task which is set before it.

BOOKS FOR REFERENCE

Standard Scales of Salaries 1927. (H.M. Stationery Office.)

Barker : *Superannuation of Teachers*. (Longmans, Green and Co.)

The Schoolmasters' Yearbook. (Dean and Sons, 1928.)